Quilting
Now & Then

Karen Willing

We offer this book to:

All the quilters and their children who inspired the pattern for this book;

Sharon Dvora and Jamie Draluck who helped bring the pieces together;

Our wonderful parents, Frank and Dena Bates, whose warmth provided the batting (and more importantly the backing!);

Sarah Morse and Chuck White whose loving hands and keen eyes brought our quilt to life;

And our husbands, Steven Willing and Charles Dock, who have provided the binding for our lives.

We offer this heirloom to our children—something for their cedar chests.

K.B.W.

J.B.D.

I dedicate the artwork in this book to the memory of Sue Dempsey whose love and encouragement prompted these illustrations.

I am grateful to my husband, Craig, who put up with my clutter, consumed more than his yearly quota of pizza, managed two very active little boys and made sure that each drawing included a cat.

Most of all, I thank the source of my creativity and life, my heavenly Father.

S.M.

Quilting
Now & Then

Written by
Karen Bates Willing
and
Julie Bates Dock

Illustrated by Sarah Morse

Now & Then Publications ✶ 725 Beach Street ✶ Ashland, OR 97520

The Johnson house is filled with colors, everywhere you gaze,
With checks and stars and polka dots—a whirling, swirling maze.

The walls aren't filled with paintings, no, it's fabric that you see.
'Cause Shirley Johnson is a quilter for her family.

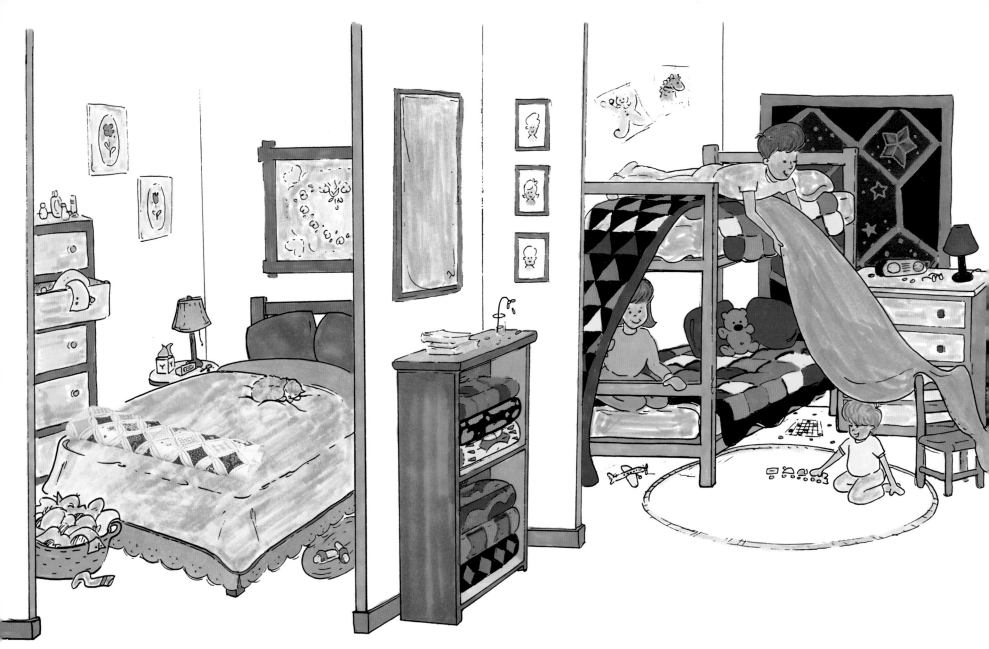

She's made a quilt for husband, Tom, it's folded on their bed.
And quilts were made for all her kids (they're Sue, and Hank, and Fred).

And Shirley has quilts piled upon each chair, and bed, and table,
And lots of quilts in progress, that she'll finish when she's able.

She likes to share her newest quilts
with people that she knows.
She also shows off old ones
made by women long ago.

Those quilts have seen her family's joys, their sorrow and their tears,
They've passed from mom to daughter over many, many years.

She cherishes these precious quilts, more ancient than the rest,
And so she stores them in a box that's called a *cedar chest*.

A cedar chest is made of wood that's from a cedar tree.
Its musty smell keeps moths away
(moths eat the quilts, you see).

One day the kids bring Charlie home
	to play with after school.
He stares at all of Shirley's quilts
	and says, "I think they're cool!

"But don't you think it's strange
	to hang a blanket on your wall?"
"Mom calls them quilts," says Sue,
	who's never questioned it at all.

"But *why* are they called quilts?" asks Charlie,
	adding one thing more:
"And what makes them so diff'rent from
	the blankets at the store?"

"A blanket's just one layer,"
　　answers Shirley, "but, you see,
A quilt has several layers.
　　If you count, you will find three."

"Please tell me how you make a quilt,"
　　says Charlie, full of wonder.
So Shirley pulls out quilts that all
　　the children snuggle under.

"And could you also tell us
　　how they made quilts long ago?"
"Did great-great-grandma Ruth make
　　quilts like you do?" "Yes or no?"

"Did *she* choose from a hundred prints
　　like you do at the store?"
"And were the quilts all sewn by hand?"
　　"And what is quilting for?"

Then Shirley hollers: "HOLD IT, KIDS!! Your questions come too fast.
I'll tell you how the quilts are made right now and in times past.

9

"Quilting's changed since grandma's day; new gadgets make it fun.
   I'll start at the beginning, so you'll learn how it was done.

"When great-great-grandma made her quilts she also sewed her clothes
   And those of all her household. That's a big job, heaven knows!

"Since she lived in the country far away from any store
A peddler sold her fabric as he travelled door to door.

"His horse-drawn cart was full of things to save a trip to town.
Along with tools and sugar, he had fabric for her gown.

"She hoarded every unused scrap when all the
        clothes were made.
    That's one way she got pieces for her quilting,
        or to trade.

            "And when the clothes seemed all worn out
                and hardly fit to wear,
            She found the parts she still could use
                and cut them out with care.

            "But if her scraps were all the same
                and she lacked something bright,
            She'd swap her fabric with her friends
                to get the mix just right.

"I don't rely on clothing scraps like she did long ago,
  And I don't have to scrimp and save from dresses that I sew.

"I pick my pattern first, instead, and find the perfect fit
  Of different colored fabrics that will soon go into it."

13

Then Charlie asks, "What patterns? I don't think I understand."
And Shirley answers, pointing to the quilts that are at hand:

"Let's see what Fred is sitting on. It's called a *Lone Star* quilt.
There's one huge central star, of tiny diamonds it is built.

"And Sue is curled inside a quilt
that's called *Sun Bonnet Sue*.

14

"And Hank, you're in a *Nine Patch* made of
squares all through and through.

"And *Grandma's Flower Garden* is the quilt that Charlie's on.
Each tiny piece has just six sides, and that's a hexagon.

Schoolhouse

Courthouse Steps

Corn and Beans

Star of Bethlehem

Turkey Tracks

Bear's Paw

"The patterns all have names that come
    from common country scenes:
The *Schoolhouse* and the *Courthouse Steps*,
    and even *Corn and Beans*.

"The Bible gave us patterns too—
    like *Star of Bethlehem*—
While nature gave us others and
    you'd guess a lot of them."

"Like *Flying Geese* and *Turkey Tracks*
    and *Bear's Paw*," Sue exclaims.
"There must be hundreds of them,
    and my mom knows all their names!"

"Well, anyway," says Shirley, "once she picked what she desired,
 A quilter cut out paper for each pattern shape required.

"The paper's called a *template*—on her fabric it would sit,
 She'd trace around its edges, careful not to jostle it.

"And when she had the shapes all marked
       she got her scissors ready.
 To cut each piece precisely she had
       hands both firm and steady.

17

"Those ladies cut each tiny piece by hand without a mutter,
But now we have a great device that's called a *rotary cutter*.

"It's like a pizza cutter with a blade both sharp and round.
It rolls through fabric layers, cutting shapes without a sound.

"And I have plastic templates that replace the paper ones.
The cutter rolls against them and the job is quickly done."

18

"Wow! What a lot of work," says Fred,
"and it's not nearly through."
"Well, now she gets out her machine,
and sews it up," says Sue.

"Yes, darling, that's what *I* do now,
but in the times long past
Great-grandma had to sew by hand.
It wasn't quite as fast.

"Yet, after many weeks and months,
with stitches small and tight,
She turned that pile of ragged scraps
into a lovely sight."

"And now she pieced the fabric that would go onto the back.
She used the largest pieces she could find within her stack.

"Between the top and bottom she would put a filling light."
"I know the stuff you mean," says Sue, "It's *batting!* Am I right?"

"Correct. The batting's like a sheet of cotton or of wool,
Or sometimes polyester, and it makes the quilt look full.

"In olden days the batting didn't come from any store.
The quilter pulled and stretched raw cotton flat upon the floor.

"Since batting was so hard to make, a quilter who was smart
Would use a tattered quilt as *batt* and give it a new start.

"The purpose is the same, no matter what the batt that's used.
It traps warm air inside the quilt. The layers next are fused.

"The quilt top's stretched across the floor, on batting and on back,
Then all three layers must be joined with stitches large and slack.

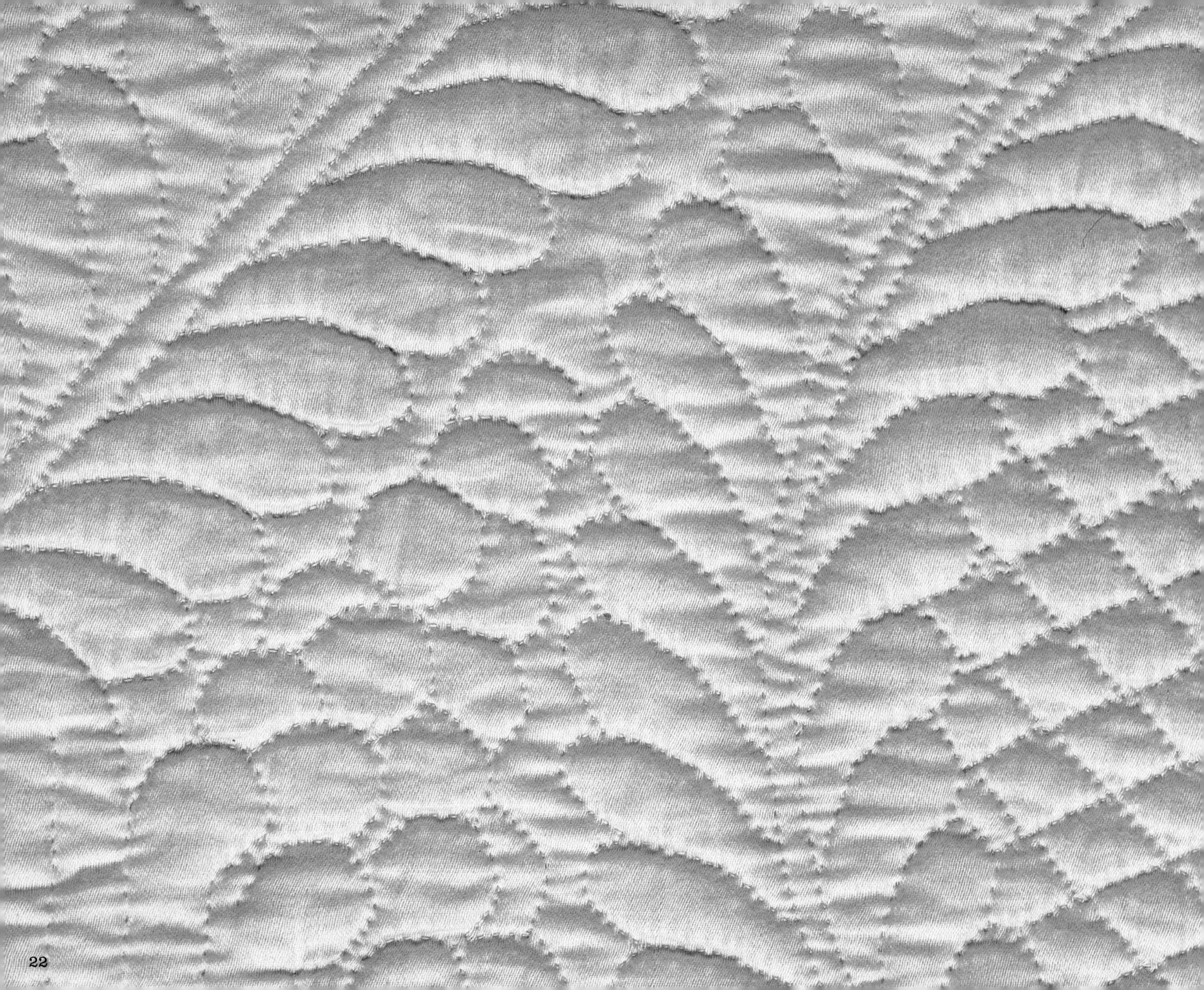

"Those stitches are called *basting*, they will hold it all in place
While tiny quilting stitches form a pattern you can trace.

"Sometimes the stitches form a leaf, a flower, or a feather.
Their job is most important for they hold the quilt together.

"I often quilt with my machine, but that's a modern way.
The early quilters sewed by hand, their quilting to display.

"The tiniest of stitches were the toughest to achieve,
But sometimes they got twenty to the inch, I do believe.

23

"The pioneers used quilting frames
to hold the layers tight
While pulling needles up and down
from morning until night.

"And sometimes at a *quilting bee*
the women got together
To quilt their tops beneath the trees
if it was sunny weather.

"The women shared both food and talk
while quilting all the day,
But children had a lot more fun—
beneath the quilts they'd play.

"This work was quite important,
for the ladies all knew well
That quilts were needed for their warmth
in winter when snow fell.

"And so young girls were taught to sew. As early as age four
A girl would thread the needles and she soon was doing more.

"For by the time she got engaged, a young girl's cedar chest
Should store a dozen finished quilts—and now she'd quilt her best

"Her bridal quilt showed off the skills
she'd practiced day and night.
The quilting shone all by itself—
the quilt was *white on white*.

"Today at special quilt shows folks can come from far and wide
To see fantastic modern quilts and old ones, side by side.

"A very few have names or dates to tell us of their past.
But most have no such messages—they hold their secrets fast.

"And that's the reason that I add
    my signature and date
To every quilt that I complete,
    a message to relate.

"So now, you kids, go check your quilts:
    they'll tell you where and when
And why I made them for you,
    with my name in purple pen."

And when her kids are all upstairs, then Shirley, with a grin,
Uncovers her old cedar chest so she can look within.

"See, Charlie, here's a quilt that came from my great-grandma Pearl
And here is one *her* mother made when she was just a girl."

"Your quilts are neat. I sure have learned
    from what you showed to me.
"I wish I had a Lone Star quilt,"
    says Charlie longingly.

"And so you will," cries Shirley
    with a sparkle in her eye,
"I'll make you one, so let's go pick
    the fabric, you and I."

And Charlie jumps excitedly
    to think he'll have one too.
I hope you know a quilter
    who will make a quilt for you!

The End

ABOUT THIS BOOK

This book was begun a few years ago as one of a simple pair of books explaining beginnings to curious children. We wished to tell our kids how fabric is made from cotton plants, and how quilts grow from mere scraps of fabric. We chose to publish this one first because quilting is our first love; we'll get around to the other cotton-pickin' book one of these days.

The illustrations began with Sarah Morse's charming line drawings. We colored them with markers and pencils, and then applied pieces of fabric. Photographs of actual quilts were super-imposed onto the finished drawings.

The authors are grateful to the many talented quilters whose work adorns our pages. Many of the quilts were miniatures created expressly for this book. Please look closely at the quilts so that you may appreciate the handiwork of the quilters listed on the following page.

These quilts would not have sparkled without the incredible talent of our photographer, Charles S. White. His ingenuity in setting up the shots to match our artwork continually amazed us.

Jamie B. Draluck of Regent Publishing deserves our special thanks for expanding the boundaries of this book beyond our original conception. His innumerable faxes reassured us that computer printing technology could do anything we wanted—for just a few cents more per copy.

We would also like to thank Mary Ellen Hopkins and Danita Rafalovitch for encouraging us to publish, David Hopkins for directing us to the resources that made it possible, and Richard Jarel for artistic advice. Enthusiasm from countless others—quilters, teachers, children—kept us going and we are grateful to them all.

Our children will howl if we do not acknowledge them by name. In chronological order, we thank Jordan, Jonathan, Shayna and Marni Willing for their patience and advice while Mom sewed and colored; and we thank two-year-old Abigail Dock for the few naps she actually took during the writing of this book.

We hope to do it again—every now and then.

Karen Bates Willing & Julie Bates Dock

QUILT CREDITS

Carol Balone: Nine Patch, 18" x 22", p. 15; Log Cabin, 2" x 3", p. 28.

Leslee M. Cramer: Trip Around the World, 18" x 20", front cover & pp. 21, 24, 30;
    Doll Applique, 18" x 18", p. 7.

Della Dearing: Cathedral Windows, 14" x 16", p. 4; One Patch, 18" x 18", p. 6.

Denise Yates Gelb: Sun Bonnet Sue, 16" x 20", pp. 9, 14.

Linda Richardson Goines: Kaleidoscope, 28" x 28", p. 28.

Martha Lewis: Double Irish Chain, 24" x 28", pp. 5, 6.

Karen Willing: Ohio Star, 20" x 26", p. 3; Churn Dash, 22" x 29", pp. 5, 6;
    Broken Dishes, 13" x 15", pp. 6, 30; Lone Star, 15" x 15", pp. 8, 14;
    Grandmother's Flower Garden, 17" x 23", pp. 9, 15, 29;
    Log Cabin, 25" x 25", p. 13; Bow Tie, 24" x 30", p. 13;
    Sampler, 31" x 34", p. 16; Giant Dahlia, 19" x 21", p. 20.

Unknown quilter: antique quilt, ca. 1930, 70" x 72", pp. 22-23.

ISBN 0-9641820-0-9

ISBN 0-9641820-1-7 (pbk)

Printed in Hong Kong

For additional copies, send $12.95 (hardback) or $8.95
(paperback) plus $3.00 for postage and handling to:

Now & Then Publications
725 Beach Street
Ashland, Oregon 97520
or FAX (541) 482-7937